AF344661

Resilient Souls & Colliding Hearts

Melinda Medina

BookLeaf Publishing

India | USA | UK

Resilient Souls & Colliding Hearts © 2024
Melinda Medina

All rights reserved.

No part of this publication may be reproduced, stored in a retrieval system, or transmitted, in any form or by any means, electronic, mechanical, photocopying, recording or otherwise, without the prior written permission of the presenters.

Melinda Medina asserts the moral right to be identified as author of this work.

Presentation by *BookLeaf Publishing*

Web: www.bookleafpub.com

E-mail: info@bookleafpub.com

ISBN: 9789363305014

First edition 2024

*For the special connections that have been with
me on various journeys through this lifetime,
those that mirror my soul and ignite a fire
within me that transcends time and space. In
every twist and turn, your presence is felt,
guiding me toward growth and deeper
understanding. Together, we dance through the
chaos of life, forever connected in a beautiful,
transformative bond. -With Love Always, M.M.
Sol*

ACKNOWLEDGEMENT

This collection would not have come to life without the support and encouragement of the incredible individuals who have accompanied me and supported me through my messy journey. I extend my heartfelt gratitude to everyone in my life whose unwavering love and belief in me inspire every word I write, especially my partner and son.

A special thanks to my educators and mentors who have shaped my understanding of the power of words and the importance of storytelling.

To the readers, thank you for being open to this exploration of love, resilience, and the human experience. Your support breathes life into my work, and I hope these poems resonate with you as deeply as they do with me.

Lastly, I dedicate this collection to all the resilient souls and kindred spirits who inspire us daily. Together, we navigate this beautifully messy journey called life.

With gratitude,

M.M. Sol

PREFACE

In the quiet moments between life's chaos and the serenity of introspection, poetry has always been my sanctuary. Resilient Souls & Colliding Hearts is a testament to the journey of navigating love, resilience, and the complex and beautifully messy human experience.

In these pages, you will find a symphony of emotions—love in its many forms, the strength found in vulnerability, the empowerment that comes from self-reflection, and what it means to be connected to others in a deeply meaningful way. Each poem is a piece of my heart, offered to you with the hope that it will resonate, offer comfort, inspire, and perhaps even heal.

This collection is about our shared human experience. It is for anyone who has ever felt the warmth of love, the sting of heartbreak, the struggle for self-acceptance, and the joy of discovering their inner strength. My words are an invitation to explore these universal themes and to find solace and empowerment within them.

As you read, I encourage you to embrace your own journey, to celebrate your resilience, and to cherish the connections that light up your path. Let this book be a reminder that no matter how messy life gets, there is beauty and strength in every twist and turn. I want you to remember that it is through connections and reflections that we find our way.

Thank you for joining me on this poetic journey. May Resilient Souls & Colliding Hearts be a companion as you find your way through the human experience.

With love,

M.M. Sol

When Souls Intertwine

You feel like oxygen
During deprivation,
Like the warmth of the sun
On a cold winter day.
Like the ocean's waves
As the sun shines its rays.

Like a deep breath
Filling collapsed lungs,
Like a smile on a face
That has long forgotten how to.
Like an embracing hug
For a body untouched.

Like an orgasm
After celibacy,
Like the moon, full and bright,
A reminder that darkness has light.
Like the release from shoulders
That have held the weight of the world,
Like the moment two soulmates meet again
After being apart for far too long.

You feel like peace
After war,

Tranquility after chaos,
The calm to my storm.
Like a stomach filled and satiated
After going unfed and fasting.

Like the climax in stories
After suspenseful waiting,
Like water quenching thirst
After days in the desert.
You feel like eyes closed
After a long day,
Like a warm shower
Cleansing dirt away.

Like a gift held onto,
Finally opened.
Though you may sail away,
This port will remain open.
Though you may fly free,
You shall return when your wings need rest.

For my soul has intertwined with yours,
Created to withstand tests.
Time is not linear.
Even if it's not this lifetime,
Maybe we will be in each other's arms
In the next.

Tango of Twin Flames

Your soul pulls me in,
Like my reflection in the mirror,
My twin.
I knew you the moment our gazes met,
A soul among eight billion others,
I didn't know lied awake yet.

I found you in my dreams,
In lifetimes past,
In worlds where I was yours,
And you were mine.
Karmic ties, destined to seek and find,
Teach me about myself,
Explore the parts I often hide.

Heal me from within,
So my external world reflects my dreams.
Whisper sweet nothings,
That mean everything.
Lessons wrapped in introspection,
Only we would understand.

A dance between the divine feminine and
masculine,
A cosmic scheme meant to be grand.

Release me to fly free,
But always come find me again.

Tangle of Love

In a tangle of love's tumultuous flow,
a water valve twists, reluctant to go.
Its metal groans with the weight of the past,
as memories rush by, too fast and too vast.

Each turn of the lever, a hesitant plea,
to halt the flood of emotions set free.
Yet the current persists, relentless and strong,
fulfilling the heart's desire for what it's longed.

In the dance of love and fiery desire,
the valve struggles to douse the consuming fire.
They've maintained silence, longing for more,
the valve turns, the floodgates open wide.

The heart yearns, as water rushes swift and wild,
free from the chains of the past, unchained and
styled.
A future unknown, vast and untamed,
treading water, the lover remains unnamed.

Wondering if it's worth the trial,
having bid love adieu, yet the echoes still rile.
Water flows gentle, kind and true,
the lover finds items they never knew.

A world without the warmth it provides,
in their embrace, love's essence resides.

Cracked Open

Penetrated, you entered each crevice of my
mind,
body, and soul, a connection so entwined.
Unbound, enamored by a single chance we met,
a lock now tampered; our paths forever set.

Exposed, fully showing—intellectual, beautiful,
making love through words, some deeply
unspoken.
A spark ignited, now a fire so bright,
leaking out desires, in the softest of light.

For all we are and all we are not,
our attempts to move are tied to this spot.
Feed me the truth, for lies I cannot bear,
create safety, love me, and always be there.

In this fleeting moment, let our spirits soar,
unveiled and free, just you and me, forevermore.

Safe Haven

Speak freely. Be free.
Your mind, body, and soul are safe,
Here with me.
I cannot create more time,
For I am not its creator.
But I can create safety.
A sanctuary where you and I,
Can be simply ourselves.

I can carve out space for you,
To feel and be seen,
Naked and exposed,
Embracing all our vulnerabilities.
I see the passion in your words,
Feel your heartache over your fears,
Hear you in your silence,
Sense you when you're not near.

I understand your duality,
The need for solace and peace,
Yet the urge to let your wings fly free.
The longing to explore the world,
And all its wonders.
The desire to dive deep,
Into your workings of your inner self.

To be loved in all your ways,
In the versions you present,
And those you keep hidden.
In all your imperfections,
To be heard and listened to,
Without the need for translation,
I appreciate all of you.

Chasing Euphoria

Euphoria, the excitement builds,
Happiness instilled, a heart fulfilled.
Engrained in choices, between expectation and
free will,
Lost in temptation, chasing the thrill.

Sensation rising, vibrations soar,
Wrapped in your arms, I crave nothing more.
Removing barriers, tearing down walls,
In your embrace, I find no limits at all.

Don't pause—there's no room for hesitation,
Your words, a melody, ignite my sensation.
Breathing deep, we seek intimacy,
How deep do your crevices go? Let me see.

Holding it in, don't let it explode;
I've captured your heart; now it's mine to
unfold.
You tried to keep it hidden, but I see it true,
Living in the moment; these days are few.

You didn't mean to slip, but I captured you,
Catapulted into me, defying what's due.

Your eyes searching for reason, unsure of the
view,
Stay a little longer; this moment's for two.

Timeless, our spirits are beautifully entwined,
A heart that beats in tandem with mine.
Don't close your eyes; let's savor the climb.
We'll linger in bliss; let's not run out of time.

Awakening to Reality

The intertwining of life journeys,
Hands clasped,
Together on this path.
Deep breaths.
Just breathe.

Here in this moment,
With you and me.
Souls reflecting,
On all that is,
And what can be.

Plot twists,
And climaxes,
Of life's trajectory.
Sharing fears,
kisses, and dreams.

Embracing in the twilight,
Lost in the reverie.
Don't leave.
Me falling for you,
You falling for me.

Hearts skipping beats.

Dancing to love's melody.
Wake up.
We must retreat.
Back to reality.

Gravity

You pull me in,
a force drawing my body near.
No matter how high I jump,
how much I try to pull away,
you keep me grounded,
feet firmly planted.

I can run, fuss, and fight,
to no avail. My body becomes weighted,
yet my heart feels frail,
drawn to your center, your core.
I long to understand your depths,
the deepest parts of the Earth that is yours.

This lover's dance keeps my planets at bay,
responsible for the push and pull,
like the tidal waves of our kindred spirits.
If you did not exist,
I would simply float away,
hitting the ground never losing contact.

Energy, effort, strength, inertia—
all go into every step to pull away,
to withdraw, flee, retreat.
Your force is simply too strong,

I am guaranteed defeat.

Gravitational pull towards each other
renders all attempts obsolete.
You are the force I have come to meet.
For I cannot escape, gravity.

Tug of War

Pull away. We tried.
Hide. Seek. Goodbye.
Hello again. Go back.
Come here. Far. I want you near.

Silence I long to hear,
forget, remember. Push, draw closer.
Sobriety. Addicted. Hang up, call again.
Twin flames? Lovers? Friends?

Can't be. Want. Need. Look at me.
Don't see. Open heart. Cut the link.
Daydream. No, don't think.
At war. Be my peace.

Unsatiated & Awakened

Holding tight to a dream,
As it floats by,
Whisking away like flower petals on a Fall
night.
Darkness,
Where there was once light.

Where there was once warmth,
There is only cold that can be found.
Where there was once love,
Now only a stranger is around.

Downgraded from beautiful dreams
To a dystopian reality.
Hopes that once soared high,
Now lie broken, beneath the sky.

How did this come to be?
One-sided effort,
A simple lack of consistency.
Aren't fantasies supposed to be full of
possibility?

Bound by a touch-free space,
Temptation leaves a lonely trace,

Craving what we can't embrace,
Hidden beneath a secret lace.

I have empty hands and a weary heart,
Wondering why we drift apart.
Yet you continue to take all I have to give,
A burning question, what am I left with?

Feeding you,
Insatiable.
Yet here I am, hungry,
Perpetually unsatiated.

We know what is at stake.
Are these fragments enough to continue to
partake?
Was I asleep before?
Now, I'm finally awake.

Unreachable

I've traced the constellations of your absence,
mapping stars that scatter in a night
I can never own, a sky beyond my reach.
Your laughter, a ghost I chase in shadows,
my heart a pilgrim in the desert of longing.

Each whisper of your name is a storm
that tears through my quiet, leaving me
to rebuild dreams from fragments of desire,
puzzling together pieces of a love
that exists in the echo of my own heartbeat.

You're a promise carved in the sand,
erased by the tide before I can touch
the contours of your closeness.
The more I reach, the more I fall
into the abyss of a beautiful illusion.

I love you like the sun loves the dawn,
unseen, unfulfilled, a fire in the sky
that warms the world but can't touch
the skin it adores. In my own universe,
you are both a star and a myth.

In the mirror of my longing,

I see the reflection of your unattainability,
a truth as sharp as the night is long,
and I hold the shards of this love
like glass, fragile, and dangerous.

So, I surrender to the space between us,
a silent witness to the aching void,
knowing that loving you is a pilgrimage
through my own uncharted wilderness,
forever yearning for a horizon, I can never cross.

Lost and Found

You'll search for me in places
Where you're trying to forget.
Creeping into dreams
Where your fantasies run through your mind's
mazes
Of what life is versus what could be.
A beautiful love story,
Or a tale of tragedy.

Two hearts, two faces, a true duality,
All parts of you made whole,
All parts accepted here.
Don't hide your darkness,
For I am not easily scared away.
Don't dim your light,
I won't be blinded by your rays.
Don't close your eyes,
I will not turn away.

I know I've been known to run and chase,
But my feet are firmly grounded
Right here in front of you.
When you don't want to see me,
You try to see right through.
But energy doesn't lie,

So you continue to hide
From the vibrations of the universe,
Afraid of what message it might convey.

But if I held your hand and whispered,
"It will all be okay,"
Will you deceive me or believe me?
Share all your inner thoughts,
Bleed them on this page,
Reveal the deepest parts of you.

I have loved you in other lifetimes
And will love you in every version of yourself.
Changing faces and bodies,
The vessel doesn't matter,
Souls tied together
Will always recognize each other,
Again, and again.

The Art of Release

I'd rather experience
Painful transparency,
And radical truthfulness.

The push and pull
Ages my soul,
It grows me weary.

I choose to live in truth,
For I find it relieving,
Unveiling layers while relentlessly believing.

Strangers to lovers to friends.
A dance of souls,
An evolving mystery.

Now, what can this be?
I ask rhetorically,
The walls continue to shift, enclosing me.

Social constructs label my essence.
But I must spread my wings,
Like beautiful butterflies meant to soar free.

Feed me honesty.

Feelings sifted through a sieve,
Released because it is not meant for me.

No longer mourning the tragedy,
Of what shall not return,
Embracing solace in the reprieve.

Finding peace in what remains.
The gifts I leave others,
Shall never be in vain.

My internal light gleams rays,
Blinding those not meant for me to save.
The sun kisses my face, shining on new days.

Unburdening and unravelling,
Aspects not meant to remain.
We cannot lose what was never ours.

Some walls crumble,
While others begin to build.
But I'm no longer climbing.

I choose to be still.
In the comfort of me,
Knowing my determination and will.

For I am oxygen inhaled,
Exhaling misalignment,

Attracting what is for me with ease.

All that I desire,
Shall be abundantly available to me.
I feel at peace.

Firmly rooted in authenticity.
Reflecting on who I was,
Honoring who I am.

Anticipating who I am becoming,
Embracing who I am meant to be,
Celebrating each part of me.

An Otherworldly Love

Your love has the ability to heal,
And transcend lifetimes.
Your love is one of a kind,
One that exists simply to remind,
That once upon a time,
The Garden existed here in this place.
It's wherever you are love,
You continue to take up space.

Your love can weaken the strong,
And empower the weak.
Your love can expose the darkness in others,
And can reveal their light.
Your love is what gods and mortals have fought
for,
With all their might.
Your love is a force no one can tame or conquer,
A flame that burns ever bright.

Your love feels like peace and tranquility.
Like waves caressing the shore.
Your love pushes those to enter the depths of
their desires,
Enticing them to want more.

Your love is forgiving, relentless, and
unconditional.
A journey with a never-ending lore.
A symphony that echoes, forevermore
A lingering magic that cannot be ignored.

Your love dilutes all other loves in existence,
You entered this world with love as your
mission.
Some may crave your love like an addiction,
They may mistake your love for lust.
Confusing it with all that they are missing,
Yet there's a reason your love needs to thrive,
Your love nurtures souls, helping them feel
alive.
A force that reminds others to continue to strive.

For there is a clear distinction,
A "before" and "after" your love's embrace.
Once they have experienced you,
Their very being is never in the same place.
Your love etches memories,
Deep in their souls, hearts, and brains.
Your love never leaves others completely
unchanged.
It's like their spirit has finally become untamed.

Your love is captivating and multifaceted,
A present love never eclipsed.

Your love is unique and irreplaceable,
A deep love leaving hearts transfixed.
Your love is a timeless embrace,
A love that creates a sacred space.
Your love is an anchor that is secure,
A love that is completely pure.

Your love is a radiant spark,
A love that ignites every pleasure.
Your love is a worthy love,
A love beyond earthly measure.
Your love is unlike any other love,
A love that remains whole under pressure.
Your love is an otherworldly love,
A love that is a precious treasure.

Journey to Self-Love

Hollowed,
Emptied,
Broken—
Only to be filled,
Whole,
Healed.
The love I needed was me.

I looked in the mirror,
Forgetting all that I am,
Brought back to who I was
And who I want to be.
Led astray,
Now I'm the leader of me,
Taking back control,
No longer in the passenger seat.

A journey of introspection,
Self-reflection,
Exposing all parts of me.
Ready to meet every woman:
Who I was,
Who I am,
Who I plan to be.

Sorry, little girl,

For never feeling enough,
For never speaking up,
For holding everything in,
For taming your flame,
For always taking the blame.

Hello to the woman I am,
The woman set free,
No longer silent,
No longer a slave
To what the world wants her to be.
The woman who disrupts,
The woman who won't stay quiet,
The woman who gives love,
With an open heart and mind.

The woman you're working on
Will always take time
With your feet planted on this earth,
Use it wisely—
Until it's time to return to dirt and dust.
I'll hold your hand through it all,
It's always been you and me.

A village never to be found,
Only your shadow I see.
Don't worry—we came to this world naked,
Here for a little while and meant to be free,
On a beautiful, imperfect human journey.

Liberated Identity

Labels. What do they show? What do they
mean?
To warn, to identify, to inform,
to remain ostracized,
to be chastised for our chosen identities.
What if we don't conform?
Would they still care to see
how we choose to show up?
how we choose to show love?
how we choose to simply be?
Us, in all our versions, all deserving.

Nothing, yet all things.
We want to simply flow,
fluidity, always unique.
We don't align with normality,
can't be placed in a box,
can't be reduced to a check on a list.
Those things entrap us,
into everything we are, yet are not.
We simply cannot be trapped to this spot,
confined, held captive, waiting to be free,
released.

From apprehended,

to liberated,
from ceased,
to seized.

Echoes of the Femme Fatales

History repeats,
A woman of love,
Ostracized often for her beauty and might.
Women in tales, bold and bright,
Like Helen of Troy, whose face sparked a war,
Allure igniting envy to its core.

Cleopatra, queen of the ancient Nile,
Her intelligence and charm beguile.
Yet history paints her a seductress, sly,
A false narrative crafted to vilify.

Jezebel, in the Bible's pages,
Power and strength that make others pale,
Branded with infamy, her legacy frail,
Medea, defying norms with her fierce might,
Casted out for vengeance, her truth ignites.

They failed to understand her plight,
Medusa, a victim turned to stone,
Jealousy's grip made her stand alone.
For true beauty they feared to show,
Her lethal gaze a warning to those below.

Joan of Arc, with fiery resolve,

Condemned for her visions, a rebel involved.
Aphrodite, blessed with beauty and grace,
Scorned by others, a cruel disgrace.

Athena, exiled for her strength,
Forced into shadows, she held her length.
A succubus, with eyes ablaze,
Haunting dreams in a seductive haze.

Fulfilling desires, drawing you near,
Her touch ignites where there was once fear.
In her arms, all reason fades,
Mortals enslaved to duty's masquerade.

The price of love, a steep trial,
In the tapestry of time, they stand,
Their stories echoing through the land,
Woven and twined, a warning I bring,
For I am all-encompassing and divine,
Embodying these women, heart, soul, and mind.

Sanctuary of Stillness

Pause and breathe deeply,
Let go of the race.
Find solace in stillness,
Make peace with your pace.

In the chaos of the world,
Find your inner calm.
A sanctuary of solace,
A personal psalm.

Rest is not a weakness,
It's a time to renew.
Allow yourself to pause,
It's a gift to you.

Forgive yourself for yesterday,
And all its heavy weight.
Today is a fresh canvas,
To create something great.

Perfectly Imperfect

Complex and multifaceted,
altogether, yet unhinged.
Unhappiness becoming binged,
let the journey now begin.

Externally glowing,
my light is showing.
Peeling layers of my onion,
watering flowers, quenching thirst,
blooming as pieces are purged.

Dying, rebirthing,
perfectly imperfect,
as is the human experience.
Completed with flaws,
divine and aligned,
Connected, both heart and mind.

Unified Fragments

These versions make up a whole of me,
No need to imagine a revised version.
For I am simply me,
All-encompassing of the different parts of my
past.

All facets deserve a seat at the table,
They are all a reflection
Of everything I am,
Of everything I'll ever be.

Each moment and memory,
A piece of my story.
Each joy and sorrow,
A part of my glory.

I am the sum of my experiences,
The total of my days.
I am every triumph and trial,
Every winding maze.

I embrace my complexities,
My contradictions and grace.
For in the tapestry of my being,
Every thread has its place.

No need to seek perfection,
In the mosaic of my soul.
For in every fragment and fracture,
Lies a beautifully imperfect whole.

So here I stand, unaltered, unmasked,
A testament to my history.
All versions of me, together at last,
Embracing the harmony of my future, present,
and past.

Just Be

Be a flower in a war.
Be a light in the darkest hour.
Be a whisper of hope.

Be a breath of fresh air.
Be a touch of kindness.
Be a sunrise after the longest night.

Be heard without words.
Be felt deeply.
Be a song with a peaceful melody.

Be a mirror that reflects the beauty in others.
Be a path leading to healing.
Be a reminder of love.

Be a dreamer whose dreams have no limits.
Be everything the world is not.
Be the soul that inspires others to just be.